Animals!

Monarch
Butterflies
Up Close

Carmen Bredeson

Enslow Elementary

CONTENTS

WORDS TO KNOW

antennae (an TEN ee)—Feelers on the heads of insects. A single feeler is called an antenna.

chrysalis (KRIHS ah lihs)—The stage in a butterfly's life after it is a caterpillar. It is a firm case that does not move.

nectar (NEK tur)—Sweet juice in flowers.

poison (POY zuhn)—Something an animal eats or touches that causes sickness or death.

proboscis (proh BOZ kihs)—A tube used by butterflies for sucking nectar from flowers.

Parts of a Monarch Butterfly

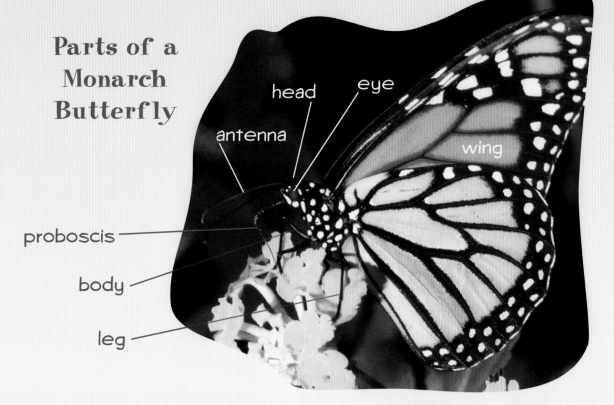

head

eye

antenna

wing

proboscis

body

leg

MONARCH BUTTERFLY

Monarch butterflies have big orange and black wings. They live in North and South America. They also live on islands in the Pacific Ocean.

MONARCH EGG

UP CLOSE

A monarch begins life as a tiny egg. Mother butterfly lays her eggs on milkweed plants. She lays hundreds of eggs, but usually only one on each leaf. Four days later, a tiny gray caterpillar comes out. It eats the eggshell, but it is still hungry.

Monarch eggs on ▶
a milkweed leaf

MONARCH CATERPILLAR

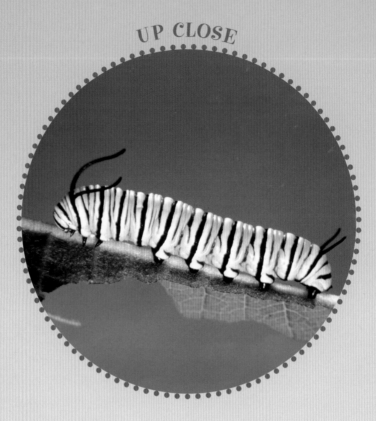

Munch, munch. The caterpillar eats some milkweed leaves. Milkweed plants are poisonous. The poison does not hurt the caterpillar. The poison makes the caterpillar taste bad to some birds and insects.

The caterpillar has yellow, black, and white stripes. These colors tell birds and some insects that the caterpillar is not good to eat.

MONARCH CHRYSALIS

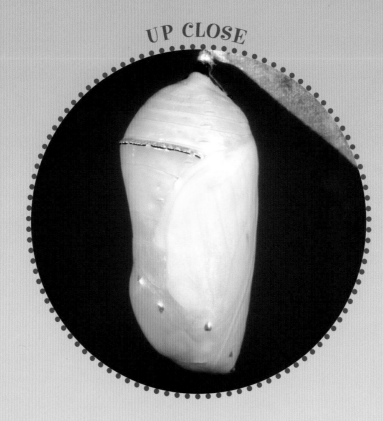

After about two weeks, the caterpillar hangs upside down from a branch. It sheds its skin and becomes a chrysalis. Then something amazing happens to the chrysalis: It starts to change into a beautiful butterfly.

MONARCH WINGS

Butterfly wings
are covered
with scales.
The scales give
butterflies their
beautiful colors.

(as seen under
a microscope)

Ten days later the butterfly pushes out of the
chrysalis case. Four orange and black wings start
to spread. The wings are wet and wrinkled. The
butterfly pumps blood into the wings. They unfold
slowly and dry in the sun. When the wings are
dry, the monarch is ready to fly.

MONARCH BODY

A butterfly has six legs and four wings on the middle of its body. This part of the body has very strong muscles. The muscles move the butterfly's legs and wings. Many monarchs fly around North and South America during warm weather.

14

MONARCH PROBOSCIS

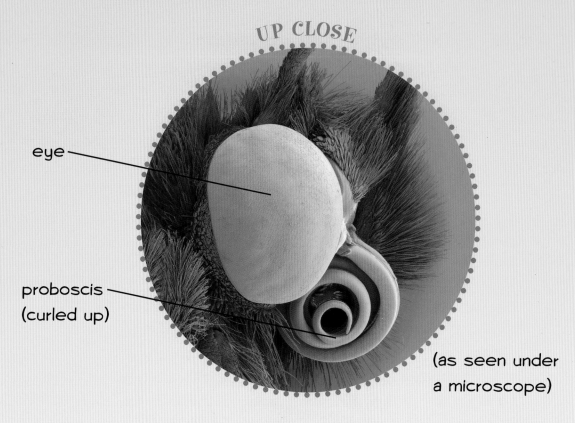

UP CLOSE

eye

proboscis
(curled up)

(as seen under
a microscope)

The butterfly flutters from flower to flower,
looking for food. It drinks the sweet juice from
flowers. This juice is called nectar. The butterfly
has a long tube called a proboscis. It is shaped
like a straw. *Slurp. Slurp.* The nectar goes up
the proboscis.

proboscis

MONARCH ANTENNAE

UP CLOSE

A monarch's head has two big eyes and two
antennae. The hair-like antennae wave in the air.
Each one has a little round ball on the end. The
antennae help the butterfly smell and feel.

eye

MONARCH CLAWS

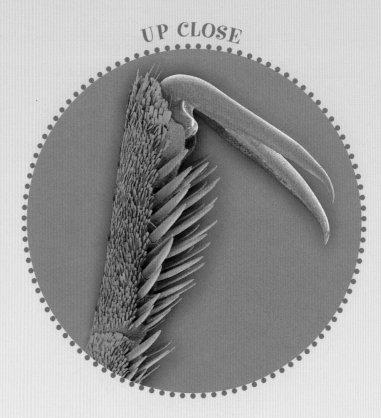

UP CLOSE

Cool weather comes. Monarchs fly to mountains in Mexico. They fly to trees near the ocean in California. Tiny claws on their feet grab tree branches. The monarchs sleep and rest until spring. Then it is time to fly home again. Bye-bye, butterfly.

Monarchs cling to ▶ a tree in Mexico.

LIFE CYCLE

Egg 3-7 days

Caterpillar
9-15 days

Butterflies live 2-6 weeks
in summer, or 7-8 months if
they are monarchs that fly
south in winter.

Chrysalis
8-14 days

LEARN MORE

BOOKS

Eckart, Edana. *Monarch Butterfly*. Danbury, Conn.: Children's Press, 2005.

Rockwell, Anne. *Bugs are Insects*. New York: Harper Trophy, 2001.

Sutton, Paul. *Eyewitness: Butterfly and Moth*. New York: Dorling Kindersley Publishing, 2000.

WEB SITES

Animal Facts: The Monarch Butterfly.
  <http://www.kidzone.ws/animals/monarch_butterfly.htm>

Enchanted Learning.
  <http://www.enchantedlearning.com/subjects/butterfly/species/Monarch.shtml>

Monarch Lab.
  <http://www.monarchlab.org>

INDEX

Series Literacy Consultant:
Allan A. De Fina, Ph.D.
Past President of the New Jersey Reading Association
Professor, Department of Literacy Education
New Jersey City University
Jersey City, New Jersey

Science Consultant:
Karen Oberhauser, Ph.D.
Monarch Researcher and Professor
Department of Fisheries, Wildlife, and Conservation Biology
University of Minnesota

Note to Parents and Teachers: The **Zoom In on Animals!** series supports the National Science Education Standards for K–4 science. The Words to Know section introduces subject-specific vocabulary words, including pronunciation and definitions. Early readers may need help with these new words.

Enslow Elementary, an imprint of Enslow Publishers, Inc.

Enslow Elementary® is a registered trademark of Enslow Publishers, Inc.

Library of Congress Cataloging-in-Publication Data

Bredeson, Carmen.
    Monarch butterflies up close / Carmen Bredeson.— 1st ed.
        p. cm. — (Zoom in on animals!)
    Includes index.
    ISBN 0-7660-2494-6 (hardcover)
    1. Monarch butterfly—Juvenile literature. I. Title. II. Series
QL561.D3B74 2006
595.78'9—dc22
                                                  2005020034

Enslow Elementary
an imprint of
 Enslow Publishers, Inc.
40 Industrial Road
Box 398
Berkeley Heights, NJ 07922
USA
    http://www.enslow.com

Printed in the United States of America

10 9 8 7 6 5 4 3 2 1

To Our Readers: We have done our best to make sure all Internet Addresses in this book were active and appropriate when we went to press. However, the author and the publisher have no control over and assume no liability for the material available on those Internet sites or on other Web sites they may link to. Any comments or suggestions can be sent by e-mail to comments@enslow.com or to the address on the back cover.

Photo Credits: © 2005 Frans Lanting/www.lanting.com, p. 21; © 2006 Jupiterimages Corporation, p. 3; © agefotostock/SuperStock, pp. 14, 18; © Dennis Kunkel Microscopy, Inc., pp. 12, 20; © Dr. Dennis Kunkel/Visuals Unlimited, p. 16; © Mary Holland, pp. 4–5, 9, 11, 13, 22 (caterpillar); Arthur Morris/Visuals Unlimited, pp. 1, 17, 22 (butterfly); Breck P. Kent/Animals Animals, p. 7; Edward Kinsman/Photo Researchers, Inc., p. 15; Patti Murray/Animals Animals, pp. 6, 10, 22 (egg, chrysalis); Raymond Mendez/Animals Animals, p. 8; Scott W. Smith/Animals Animals, p. 19.

Cover Photos: *left:* Arthur Morris / Visuals Unlimited; *insets top to bottom:* Patti Murray / Animals Animals; © Mary Holland; © Dr. Dennis Kunkel / Visuals Unlimited.